I am happy and grateful for this new day,
I have a choice to start again.

Today is a new opportunity for me to be better, do better and try one more time.

In faith and love I am abundant.
~ Samantha C-Panopoulos

TheWellnessUniverse.com
'Walk Away Feeling Better'

The
GRATITUDE
Affirmations

Your Daily Guide to Abundance

Author
SAMANTHA CERVINO P.

Copyright © 2018 Samantha Cervino P. and SMB Alternative Healing and Coaching

All rights reserved. This book or any portion thereof may not be reproduced or used in any manner whatsoever without the express written permission of the publisher except for the use of brief quotations in a book review.

I am grateful for my son who is the light in my life and the greatest gift and blessing God gave me.

I am grateful for my mom whose love and support is with me always.

I am grateful for my mentors and friends whose continuous support and advice assisted me in publishing this book.

Samantha Cervino P.

This Book Is for You

You are a child of this abundant Universe and there is nothing in this world you cannot have.

In this book I will guide you with daily affirmations and gratitude so you will rightly ask for what you desire, and be ready to receive the blessings that await you.

These are daily affirmations to use with gratitude in your heart for a new blessed abundant life. Every morning, read these affirmations and make a list of your own of ten things and people that add joy to your life.

Gratitude is an important attitude to acquire in your life and the most life-changing. It helps fight off negative feelings.

Gratitude shifts your thoughts from negative to positive; it changes your attitude so that you feel happy and more enthusiastic!

This puts you in a better mood and higher vibration, which in turn will attract into your life more of the things and situations you want.

How?

Because you are now putting your energy and redirecting your thoughts to the positive that surrounds you.

You are love and you are loved.
You are never alone.

The Gratitude Affirmations

Gratitude for Good Health

"I am so happy and grateful for my healthy body and mind."

Always be grateful for your health. Even if you are not feeling well, you take care of your mind by affirming you are in good health.

As you say this affirmation for good health, visualize yourself as a healthy being. Imagine you are walking outside, enjoying the beautiful weather, admiring nature and its perfection.

Picture in your mind all the things you would enjoy doing in your healthy body.

Understand that an illness cannot occur or live in the body of a healthy, positive mind.

This is a very important daily affirmation.

Gratitude for Work and Career

"I am so happy and grateful now that I am living my life purpose. I am doing what I love and making a great living."

Whatever it is you desire to be, be it.

This gratitude and affirmation is the beginning in making your dream job a reality.

Be specific on what you want, and write your own affirmation describing your ideal job, position, or next career move. Then affirm you have attained it and are living it now.

Gratitude for Money

"I am so happy and grateful now that I attract riches and wealth into my life on a consistent basis."

The Universe is abundant. It is an infinite source of supply and there is no reason why you should experience lack of any kind.

Be grateful for the riches you possess and affirm that you are always attracting more and more.

Money is circulation; it is used and designed to have, to share, to give.

It makes life easier, pays for food, clothing, study programs, children's education, helping humanity in need.

Money is great and helpful.

Gratitude to LET, and Stop Controlling

"I am so happy and grateful now that I let God/Universe/Divine guide me each day and I allow what is right for me to flow freely into my life."

This gratitude and affirmation helps you let go and freely accept what the Universe intends for you to have at this moment.

This affirmation asks that you have faith and stop controlling situations and outcomes in your life.

Just LET, and be free.

Gratitude for a Relationship

"I am so happy and grateful now that I am in a loving, committed relationship with a man/woman who loves me, respects me, inspires me, motivates me, accepts me for whom I truly am, and adds joy to my life."

If you are looking for the right person who will be your loving other half,
then this is the affirmation for you!

You can add more details.

Describe this person and visualize yourself being already in this wonderful,
loving relationship.

Feel what it would be like to be with your partner, conversations you would have, places you would visit together, etc.

Gratitude for Wisdom & Self-Acceptance

"I am so happy and grateful for my wisdom, and for my growing knowledge and understanding of myself and others. I am now accepting of myself because I understand and know who I am."

Look inside of yourself and accept what you see and how you feel. Let go of any dislikes and self-doubt.

Understand that you are a spiritual being experiencing life in a physical body.

Learn from your past experiences and don't let those define who you are today.

Gratitude for Forgiveness

"I am so happy and grateful now that I have forgiveness in my heart for myself and others and I let go of any negative feelings attached to this situation."

This gratitude and affirmation for forgiveness will help you to let go of any negative thought and feeling toward yourself and others, and for anything that caused you discomfort and pain.

Visualize yourself forgiving those who you think did you wrong, and also forgive yourself for any part you think you may have had in this situation.

Gratitude for Abundance

"I am so happy and grateful now that God's wealth flows through me in avalanches of abundance.
All my needs, desires, and wants are met.
I am one with God,
and God is everything."

This affirmation and gratitude is for an opulent life.

Know and realize that God is everything, and that you are already in possession of the wealth you desire and that are rightfully yours as a child of God.

It is through your belief that you will see.

To believe is to see.

Gratitude for a Positive Mind

"I am so happy and grateful now that I am
in control of my thoughts.
I only allow positive thoughts to enter my mind.
My thoughts are creative, loving,
and productive."

Understand that you have total control over your
mind, and the thoughts that occupy your mind.
Only allow positive thoughts in your mind.

Be aware when any negative thought enters your
mind, and right away shift that thought to
a positive one.

A negative thought will give you a negative
feeling, and your body should reject that.
It is your job to shift to a positive state whenever
you become aware of any negativity
entering your mind.

These thoughts will come in various forms such
as sadness, insecurity, doubt, fear, or jealousy.
Anything that puts you in a low vibration is
a negative thought.

About the Author

Samantha has changed and improved the lives of many people, including children with special needs, as well as countless clients in her practice of energy healing.

In addition to being an accomplished leader in her field of understanding and shifting human emotions through Reiki and EFT, she is also a blogger, published author, and motivates through her work on social media.

As a master energy healer, Samantha is committed to the personal success of her clients and is often quoted for saying:

"Life is to be felt, not planned."

A final note...

I hope you are loving this book as much as I loved writing it for you.

It is my intention that you live an abundant life, full of love, great health, and wealth.

In gratitude,

Samantha Cervino P.

SMB Alternative Healing & Coaching

samcp10@gmail.com
smbalternativehealing.me

Today, I am so happy and grateful for:

Today, I am so happy and grateful for:

Today, I am so happy and grateful for:

Today, I am so happy and grateful for:

Today, I am so happy and grateful for:

Today, I am so happy and grateful for:

Today, I am so happy and grateful for:

Made in the USA
Columbia, SC
25 August 2018